Easy Eloquence

SAMPLE THANK YOU NOTES AND SYMPATHY CARDS FOR EVERY OCCASION

SHARON PASKOFF

RANDOM HOUSE REFERENCE

NEW YORK   TORONTO   LONDON   SYDNEY   AUCKLAND

Please address inquiries about electronic licensing of any products for use on a network, in software or on CD-ROM to the Subsidiary Rights Department, Random House Information Group, fax 212-572-6003.

This book is available at special discounts for bulk purchases for sales promotions or premiums. Special editions, including personalized covers, excerpts of existing books, and corporate imprints, can be created in large quantities for special needs. For more information, write to Random House, Inc., Special Markets/Premium Sales, 1745 Broadway, MD 6-2, New York, NY 10019 or e-mail specialmarkets@randomhouse.com.

Visit the Random House Reference Web site: www.randomwords.com

Printed in the United States of America

10 9 8 7 6 5 4 3 2 1

Design by Nora Rosansky

Library of Congress Cataloging in Publication Data:

Paskoff, Sharon.
    Easy eloquence : sample thank you notes and sympathy cards for every occasion/Sharon Paskoff.
        p. cm.
    ISBN: 978-0-375-72199-1 (alk. paper)
        1. Thank-you notes. 2. Condolence notes. I. title.

BJ2115.T45P37 2007
395.4—dc22   2006048719

Dedication

Easy Eloquence is a reference book for everyone who values personal connections. Expressions of sympathy, helping hurting hearts heal, or an appreciative thank you note, strengthen the ties of family and community.

As a blessed mother of two and wife to my one and only, this book is dedicated to me, and all other carpool driving, grocery store shopping, telephone call making, kid command calling, homework helping, holiday planning, dirty laundry doing, dishwasher stacking, multi-meal managing . . . MOMS—who pursue a passion.

A Special Thanks to my parents:
Matile and Kenneth Ginburg
Who taught all of us not to sweat the little things.

Table of Contents

General Gifts

WHAT DO YOU DO WHEN: THE COLOR IS ALL WRONG, you know it is too small and you haven't worn flannel since college? Is it really the thought that counts? Yes! When someone is kind enough to give you a gift, their generosity and good intentions should be rewarded with an enthusiastic thank you note.

ETIQUETTE GUIDELINES FOR GIFTS

IT IS NEVER WRONG TO SEND A THANK YOU NOTE, IN ADDITION TO YOUR VERBAL APPRECIATION.

1. Send the note promptly, within ten days. When a gift is received by mail or UPS, the person needs to know as soon as possible that their gift arrived.
2. Be specific. Always mention the gift by name.
3. Be sincere. Use words with which you are comfortable.
4. When the gift is money, state what you will do or buy with the money.

DATE

Dear Amy and Jeff,

The gold and yellow daffodils you sent me are brightening up my room and warming my spirits. You were so kind to think of me and aid my recovery with your beautiful gift.

I am feeling better every day and hope to see you again soon. I appreciate your kindness, good wishes, and generous spirit.

Fondly,

Sharon

DATE

Dear Aunt Julia,

Thank you for the beautiful plate from the Metropolitan Museum of Art Store.

The color and design you chose will go beautifully in our kitchen. It is so pretty and adds that special touch to brighten up the whole room. James and I appreciate your kindness and thoughtful gift.

Love,

Rebecca

DATE

Dear Rosie and Jimmy,

Thank you for the beautiful housewarming gift. The blue and white floral design bowl is the perfect accent piece for the den. You have wonderful taste and always seem to know what I like. I appreciate your kindness and your helping me with the decorating details.

I hope to see you soon.

Love,

Karen

DATE

Dear Rob and Carol,

The fruit basket you sent us is beautiful and delicious. I put it on the kitchen table where we can easily help ourselves to a juicy snack. All of us love the Granny Smith apples, red plums, and pears.

Thank you for thinking of us. We greatly appreciate your thoughtfulness.

Fondly,

The Gibson Family

DATE

Dear Aunt Katheryn,

The blouse you sent me for my birthday is the perfect addition to my wardrobe. The smooth silk fabric feels great, and the color looks beautiful with my black suit. I am wearing it to a dinner party tonight and will enjoy it on many other occasions.

Thank you for thinking of me on my birthday. Your thoughtful gift made it an extra special day.

Love,

Sharon

DATE

Dear Angela,

Your gift was such a pleasant surprise. You picked the perfect cologne. The spice fragrance is so enjoyable that I look forward to wearing it every day. It was thoughtful of you to think of me. I appreciate your kindness, and am very lucky to have a friend like you.

Maybe next week we can get together for a movie. I look forward to seeing you soon.

Your friend,

Brian

DATE

Dear Aunt Millie,

The sweater you gave me is beautiful and will keep me warm all winter. I love the soft grey color—it goes with everything. The classic design is so comfortable that I will enjoy wearing your beautiful gift often.

Thank you for giving me such a lovely present. I hope you have a wonderful holiday season.

Best regards,

Rebecca

DATE

Dear Craig,

The book you sent me could not have come at a more perfect time. I am going away for the weekend, and I wanted something good to read. This book has had great reviews and will keep me entertained for hours. I am really looking forward to reading it.

Your kindness is one of your many wonderful qualities, and I am very lucky to have a friend like you. Thank you for thinking of me.

Best regards,

Steve

DATE

Dear Barbara and Jerry,

Thank you for the subscription to "Time" magazine. I will enjoy reading your thoughtful gift and keeping up with current events. Now that I am retired, I will be reading "Time" at the lake while waiting for the fish to bite!

I appreciate your generous spirit and friendship.

All the Best,

Robert

DATE

Dear Aunt Molly,

Thank you for the subscription to "Sports Illustrated." You have given me the perfect birthday present! I will enjoy the magazine all year by keeping up with my favorite teams and latest sports news. Whenever "Sports Illustrated" arrives I will think of you. I am very lucky to have such a sweet and thoughtful aunt.

Love,

John

DATE

Dear Aunt Julia and Uncle Robert,

Thank you for the handsome tie. The subtle blue and yellow geometric design on silk fabric will be a big hit at my office or when I go out to dinner. The tie's timeless elegance will always be in style and a favorite of mine to wear.

I appreciate your thinking of me with such a beautiful gift.

Love,

Mason

DATE

Dear Nancy,

Thank you for the silver and green pen. Its sturdy construction and comfortable design will make writing at work or home, a pleasure. The unique color combination adds variety to my conservative pen collection. I only wish it could improve my handwriting!

I appreciate your thinking of me with such a useful and handsome gift.

All the Best,

Steve

DATE

Dear Bobby,

Thank you for the Atlanta Braves tickets. It was a beautiful day and the seats were great. I have always wanted to sit right behind home plate to get a good look at the pitchers. Carol and I had a good time at Turner Field, eating hot dogs and cheering on the Braves.

I appreciate your thinking of us. We really enjoyed the day.

All the Best,

William

DATE

Dear Laura,

I love the spa gift set you sent me for my birthday. The lavender soap, soft scented candles, and loofa mitt are the perfect combination for relaxing in the bath. I plan on spoiling myself every day.

Thank you for thinking of me with such a lovely gift and helping me celebrate my birthday.

All the Best,

Mary

DATE

Dear Uncle George,

Thank you for the wallet and birthday good wishes. The brown leather wallet is good looking and the perfect size for my pocket. Also, there is plenty of room for my credit cards, identification information, and dollar bills. You were so kind to remember me, and I hope to see you when I come home in December.

Love,

$\mathcal{O}$RGANIZATION, ORGANIZATION, ORGANIZATION

	FROM	DATE RECEIVED	GIFT DESCRIPTION	NOTE MAILED ✓
1.				
2.				
3.				
4.				
5.				
6.				
7.				
8.				
9.				
10.				
11.				
12.				

ORGANIZATION, ORGANIZATION, ORGANIZATION

FROM	DATE RECEIVED	GIFT DESCRIPTION	NOTE MAILED ✓
1.			
2.			
3.			
4.			
5.			
6.			
7.			
8.			
9.			
10.			
11.			
12.			

$\mathcal{O}$RGANIZATION,
ORGANIZATION, ORGANIZATION

	FROM	DATE RECEIVED	GIFT DESCRIPTION	NOTE MAILED ✓
1.				
2.				
3.				
4.				
5.				
6.				
7.				
8.				
9.				
10.				
11.				
12.				

Weddings

THE GIFT WAS WRAPPED BEAUTIFULLY—crisp white paper with an elegant violet wired ribbon and baby's breath to remind my friend that she was a bride-to-be. Aunt Doris had brought it over herself for my friend and her mom to unwrap in her presence. When the top of the box came off, it took our breath away. We were gasping for breath to stall for time, because neither of us knew exactly what it was! Thankfully, Aunt Doris went on and on with her story about her lengthy search to find the perfect wedding gift—parking lot woes, mall mania, and a sales clerk's inappropriate dress. From her shopping expedition tale, we were able to detect clues about the gift's identity.

What do you do if you do not like the gift, are not sure what it is, and only want to know where to return it? If it would hurt Aunt Doris's feelings to show how you really feel, you obviously put a smile on your face, compliment the color, size, design, thank her again and again, and applaud the effort.

ETIQUETTE GUIDELINES FOR WEDDINGS

BEFORE YOU CAN LIVE HAPPILY EVER AFTER, YOU MUST
WRITE YOUR THANK YOU NOTES!

1. All wedding gifts require a thank you note, even when you have expressed verbal appreciation.
2. Notes should be written as gifts are received. However, the bride and groom can take up to three months to write a thank you note.
3. The bride usually sends the thank you notes because she receives most of the gifts.
4. The bride should sign her name, but mention the groom's name in the note.
5. It is fine for the groom to write and sign a note, mentioning the bride's name, especially if he receives the gift.
6. It is not incorrect to sign both names, but it is more acceptable to sign only one, mentioning the other person in the thank you note.
7. Be specific. Always mention the gift by name.
8. Be sincere. Express your appreciation with words with which you are comfortable.
9. When the gift is money, state what you will do with it or what you intend to buy.

DATE

Dear Mr. and Mrs. Roth,

Thank you for the beautiful silver picture frame. My favorite wedding picture is of Ben and me standing in front of the church. Your lovely frame will capture this happy moment, and you will always be in our thoughts. We appreciate your thinking of us with such a thoughtful wedding gift.

Best regards,

DATE

Dear Jay,

Thank you for the beautiful tray. I love the contemporary design. It is so colorful and functional that there are many ways Ben and I will enjoy using it. We like to have people over, and your gift will be perfect for entertaining. The next time you are in town, we will have you and the gang for dinner.

We appreciate your thinking of us and will enjoy your lovely wedding gift.

Love,

DATE

Dear Allison and Jack,

The vase you gave us is the perfect addition to our living room. I love fresh flowers, especially day lilies, and they will look beautiful in the crystal vase. It is people like you who have made our wedding so special. Thank you for the lovely gift and for celebrating our happiness with us. Ben and I appreciate your thinking of us.

Love,

Cynthia

DATE

Dear Mr. and Mrs. Whitefield,

Thank you for the place setting of Lenox china. We are looking forward to using it for our family Mother's Day brunch. Your lovely present will enhance the beauty of our table, and Ben and I will enjoy it and think of you on many occasions. You were so thoughtful to send us such a beautiful wedding gift.

Best regards,

Cynthia

DATE

Dear Aunt Marilyn and Uncle Robert,

Thank you for the beautiful place mats and napkins. The color you chose looks great. They brighten up the whole kitchen. Ben and I will enjoy using them when we sit down for coffee in the morning and when we have friends over for dinner. It was so kind of you to think of us with such a lovely and useful wedding gift.

Love,

Cynthia

DATE

Dear Debi and Stan,

Thank you for the hand painted candle-sticks. They reflect your wonderful taste and eye for design. The warm colors of the candlesticks will look great in the living room where we will keep them on the coffee table.

Ben and I appreciate your thinking of us with such a thoughtful and beautiful wedding gift.

Love,

Cynthia

DATE

Dear Aunt Bea and Uncle Seymour,

Your wedding gift arrived today, and I was so excited when I opened it. The silver serving pieces really made me feel like a bride. I have loved this silver pattern for a long time, and Ben and I will enjoy using the pieces forever.

Thank you for the wonderful wedding gift and for sharing this happy time with us.

Love,

DATE

Dear Gail and Lewis,

Thank you for the coffee maker. As you know, our days are busy from morning to night, so we need a good cup of coffee to start the day. Now with your thoughtful gift our coffee will taste great and be a pleasure to make.

Ben and I loved seeing you at the wedding and hope to see you again soon.

Best regards,

Cynthia

DATE

Dear Joan and Billy,

What a wonderful and thoughtful gift you sent us for our wedding. Cynthia and I will use the portable phone every day. It will be so helpful to have a phone outside when we are working in the yard, and convenient all over the house.

Thank you for thinking of us with such a great gift.

Best regards,

DATE

Dear Mr. and Mrs. Newman,

Thank you for your generous wedding gift. Your check is greatly appreciated because Ben and I are saving for a new house. With your thoughtful present, we will reach our down payment goal sooner than we thought.

We appreciate your thinking of us and hope to see you soon.

Best regards,

DATE

Dear Carol and Rob,

Thank you for the dozen wine glasses. Ben and I like to have a glass of wine on the patio in the evenings and watch the sun set. Now we have beautiful glasses to enhance the moment. We will enjoy your gift on many occasions and look forward to seeing you soon. Ben and I appreciate your kindness and your sharing our wedding with us.

Love,

DATE

Dear Mr. and Mrs. O'Brian,

Thank you for the beautiful serving platter. The fish design is great for entertaining. I will use the platter to serve my "famous" barbecue shrimp and for a mixture of culinary delights.

Ben and I were so happy to see you at the wedding. It meant a lot to us for you to come all the way from Boston. We appreciate your lovely gift and your sharing this happy time with us.

Fondly,

Cynthia

DATE

Dear Aunt Dorothy,

Thank you for the set of stainless steel steak knives. Your thoughtful gift is surely needed. Before your gift arrived, our assortment of knives could hardly cut through chicken. Now we are able to enjoy dinner no matter how much we overcook the meat!

The next time you are in town, please come over and we will grill some steaks on the barbecue. Cynthia and I really appreciate your thoughtful wedding gift.

Love,

Ben

DATE

Dear Aunt Gloria,

Thank you for the lovely ceramic bowl. The colors are so varied, I can use the bowl in every room. Ben and I cannot decide whether to put a beautiful blue violet plant in it or to use it as a decorative accent piece. We will enjoy it any way we use it and think of you.

We were so glad when Mom told us that you were feeling well enough to attend the wedding. The reception was fun. I know everyone enjoyed being with you. I never knew you could dance like that! Stay well, and thank you again for the wedding gift and for sharing this happy time with us.

Love,

Cynthia

DATE

Dear Mr. and Mrs. Lawrence,

Thank you for the beautiful teapot and cups. I chose our wedding china because I loved the teapot design. The soft pink roses, graceful handle, and petite shape are a delight. Ben and I will treasure your thoughtful gift and spend many quiet moments enjoying each other and our favorite tea.

We appreciate your wedding gift and the two of you celebrating our wedding with us and being a part of our lives.

Love,

Cynthia

DATE

Dear Carmen and Peter,

The antique style wedding photograph album is beautiful. I love the way it is organized by photograph size, graphic design, and personal thoughts. Putting our wedding album together will be a pleasure. Your thoughtful gift is the perfect home for all of our wedding memories.

Thank you for thinking of us, and we appreciate your kindness.

Love,

Cynthia

DATE

Dear Allison,

Thank you for the great looking guest towels. As you know, our powder room is blue and white. Your white towels with the blue butterflies are the perfect accessory to complement the room. Guests, along with Ben and I, will enjoy the soft texture and creative design.

Love,

DATE

Dear Margo and Chris,

The yellow Kitchen Aid Mixer is greatly appreciated because I love to bake and Ben enjoys desserts. The mixer is durable and will perform a variety of baking tasks. I cannot wait to use it!

You were so sweet to come all the way from Boston to celebrate our wedding. We hope you enjoyed the service, being with family, and all the parties. Thank you for being with us and for such a great wedding gift.

Love,

Cynthia

DATE

Dear Aunt Kitty and Uncle Charles,

Thank you for the silver salt and pepper shakers. The contemporary design will add interest to any table setting and it complements our china pattern.

We were sorry you were not able to attend our wedding. I was glad to hear that you are now feeling better. Ben and I are looking forward to seeing you at the beach this summer. We appreciate your good wishes, thoughtful advice, and lovely gift.

Love,

Cynthia

DATE

Dear Rosie,

You must have read my mind. A toaster oven is exactly what we wanted because of our limited kitchen counter space. Ben and I will use it every morning for breakfast toast and for many other culinary tasks. We hope you had a good time at our wedding. I know you did not miss a beat on the dance floor.

Thank you for the extremely useful toaster oven and for celebrating our wedding with us.

Love,

$\mathcal{O}$RGANIZATION,
ORGANIZATION, ORGANIZATION

FROM	DATE RECEIVED	GIFT DESCRIPTION	NOTE MAILED ✓
1.			
2.			
3.			
4.			
5.			
6.			
7.			
8.			
9.			
10.			
11.			
12.			

$\mathcal{O}$RGANIZATION,
ORGANIZATION, ORGANIZATION

	FROM	DATE RECEIVED	GIFT DESCRIPTION	NOTE MAILED ✓
1.				
2.				
3.				
4.				
5.				
6.				
7.				
8.				
9.				
10.				
11.				
12.				

Bar / Bat Mitzvah, Confirmation, Graduation

MY SON'S BAR MITZVAH WAS IN 1997. He needed to write 175 thoughtful notes to family and friends. Well, it is hard enough to get a thirteen-year-old to answer a question, pick up dirty clothes, or engage in a conversation, so how was he going to complete the thank you note task in a pleasant and timely fashion? I devised a plan to help him get organized, write the thank you notes, and understand their importance.

First, I used a lethal weapon, guilt. I explained how people had gone out of their way to purchase a gift, and possibly braved the post office to mail it. Then they took the time to attend the Bar Mitzvah, come to the party, and were kind enough to do it all gracefully. I told him, "The least you can do is write them a nice thank you note." On a note card, I gave him a few key phrases and an appropriate closing line. His thank you notes could have been more thoughtful and completed faster if he'd had this book.

ETIQUETTE GUIDELINES FOR BAR/BAT MITZVAH, CONFIRMATION, GRADUATION

DO TEN THANK YOU NOTES A DAY AND THE NUDGING WILL GO AWAY.

1. All gifts require a thank you note even if you have thanked the givers verbally, except for immediate family.

2. Notes should be written when you receive the gift. However, up to three months from the Bar/Bat Mitzvah, Confirmation, or Graduation date is acceptable.

3. In addition to saying thank you for the gift, thank people for traveling a long distance to attend. For example: "It was so kind of you to come all the way from Boston to attend my Graduation. Your being here means a lot to me."

4. If you have a party, it's nice to acknowledge someone being there or not being able to attend the party. For example, "I hope you had a good time at the party" or "I am so sorry you were not able to attend my party."

5. Be specific. Always mention the name of the gift. For example, "Thank you for the Timex sports watch in honor of my Confirmation."

6. Be sincere when expressing your appreciation by using words with which you are comfortable.

7. When the gift is money, state what you will do with it, or what you intend to buy with the money. For example, "Thank you for the Bar Mitzvah check. I am going to put it in the bank in my college fund account."

DATE

Dear Mr. and Mrs. Simon,

Thank you for the pen and pencil set. I am keeping it in my desk drawer so I can use it for homework. The pencil and pen's smooth style will make my homework neater; and that will help my homework grade.

I appreciate your thinking of me with such a useful gift.

Best regards,

Adam

DATE

Dear John,

Thank you for the American Express gift certificate. I am looking forward to buying some new DVDs with it. I hope you had fun at the party, and I appreciate your celebrating my _____ with me.

Your friend,

Adam

DATE

Dear Beth,

Thank you for the Best Buy gift certificate.
That store has so much to choose from, it will
be easy to find something I really like. The
party was a lot of fun. I hope you had a good
time.

   Again, thank you for celebrating my
_____ with me.

                                    Your friend,
                                    Sarah

DATE

Dear Jennifer,

Thank you for the Nike sports bag. My soccer bag has worn out, so I am glad to have a new one. It has plenty of room for my uniform, shoes, and ball. I appreciate your thoughtful gift and your celebrating my _____ with me.

Your friend,

Sarah

DATE

Dear Josh,

Thank you for the CD. Music helps me relax and concentrate so I'll enjoy your CD when doing my homework. I appreciate your celebrating my _____ with me.

Your friend,

Sarah

DATE

Dear Mr. and Mrs. Seigle,

Thank you for the iPod. Now, with your thoughtful gift, I can enjoy my favorite music at home, on vacation, or in the car.

My family and I appreciate your coming all the way from Boston and celebrating my _____ with us.

Best regards,

Adam

DATE

Dear Mr. and Mrs. Freeman,

Thank you for the camera. I have enjoyed taking pictures of animals for a long time. Now, with your thoughtful gift, I can improve the quality of my photography. I love the camera!

It was kind of you to come to my _____ and party. I hope you had a good time. Again, thank you for such a wonderful gift and for celebrating with me.

Best regards,

Adam

DATE

Dear Mr. and Mrs. Butler,

Thank you for the handsome black leather belt. I tried it on, and it fits great. This year I will be attending a lot of my friends' parties, so I will be wearing the belt on many occasions.

I appreciate your thinking of me and celebrating my _____.

Love,

Adam

DATE

Dear Betsy and Ellis,

Thank you for the check in honor of my
_____.Your gift will help me buy a
stereo system for my room.

I hope you had a good time at my party. I
appreciate your being there and celebrating
this happy time with me.

Love,

Adam

DATE

Dear Mr. and Mrs. Lewis,

Thank you for the beautiful book about England. The photographs are very lifelike, giving me a better understanding of what England looks like and the personality of the people. One day I hope my family will travel there.

I hope you had a good time at the party, and I appreciate your celebrating my _____ with me.

Best regards,

Adam

DATE

Dear Mr. and Mrs. Franklin,

Thank you for the U.S. Savings Bond in honor of my _____. It was thoughtful of you to think of my future with such a nice gift. I know it will help me meet my financial responsibilities some day.

I appreciate your thinking of me and celebrating this happy occasion.

Best regards,

Adam

DATE

Dear Mr. and Mrs. Silver,

Thank you for the binoculars. Dad and I will enjoy using them at baseball and football games. They are so compact, yet powerful, and they will help me see every play. There are many events where your thoughtful gift will come in handy and give me a better view.

I appreciate your coming all the way from New York and celebrating my _____ with me.

Best regards,

George

DATE

Dear Aunt Judy and Uncle Lewis,

Thank you for the beautiful monogrammed overnight bag. It is the perfect size and weight to take when I spend the night out at my friend's house. I love the brightly colored design and the monogram is a special touch.

I appreciate your thoughtful _____ gift and your celebrating this happy time with me.

Love,

Courtney

DATE

Dear Megan,

Thank you for the beautiful angel necklace. The silver design goes with everything, and it is the perfect length around my neck. Angels are fun to collect, and this will be one of my favorites.

I appreciate your thoughtful gift and your celebrating my _____ with me.

Your friend,

Sarah

DATE

Dear Mr. and Mrs. Anderson,

Thank you for the beautiful pearl earrings in honor of my _____. Pearls are my favorite because they go with every-thing. The style you picked is casual enough for school every day, but I will also enjoy wearing them out to dinner because they are so pretty.

I appreciate your coming all the way from Boston for my _____ week-end. All of us enjoyed being with you and celebrating this happy occasion together.

Love,

Sarah

DATE

Dear Aunt Michelle and Uncle Mark,

Thank you for the check in honor of my
_____. Mom and Dad
have opened a college savings account for
me, and your gift will go there. I hope to attend an out-of-state university, so all the
money I can save now is helpful.

I appreciate your thoughtful gift that will
help me reach my future academic goals. I
am sorry you were not able to attend my
_____, but I am looking
forward to seeing you the next time we are in
Boston.

Love,

Laura

DATE

Dear Mr. and Mrs. Sadler,

Thank you for the sports watch. I will use it at school to make sure I am not late for class. Also, it will come in handy when I run. I am looking forward to timing my distance in the mile, by individual laps, and overall time. The watch is great!

I hope you had a good time at my party. I appreciate your thoughtful _____ gift and that you celebrated this happy time with me.

Best regards,

George

DATE

Dear Mr. and Mrs. Singleton,

Thank you for the book, "Oh, the Places You'll Go!" by Dr. Seuss. This famous book is full of inspiration for all ages. I will enjoy its entertaining story and fun illustration.

I appreciate your gift and celebrating my graduation with me.

Best regards,

Adam

DATE

Dear Mr. and Mrs. Johnson,

Thank you for the donation to the Genesis Shelter in honor of my _____.
Your gift touched my heart and reminded me we are all part of a community that needs our help. I am glad to know the children at the Genesis Shelter will benefit from your gift.

I appreciate your generous spirit, community awareness, and honoring me in such a beautiful way.

Love,

Sarah

DATE

Dear Virginia,

Thank you for the lovely stationery. The bright blue and green colors will inspire me to write letters to family and friends. This summer I will use it to keep in touch with my best friend when we are out of town. It was great to see you last weekend at my _____. I hope you will visit us again soon.

Your friend,

Sarah

$\mathscr{O}$RGANIZATION,
ORGANIZATION, ORGANIZATION

	FROM	DATE RECEIVED	GIFT DESCRIPTION	NOTE MAILED ✓
1.				
2.				
3.				
4.				
5.				
6.				
7.				
8.				
9.				
10.				
11.				
12.				

ORGANIZATION, ORGANIZATION, ORGANIZATION

	FROM	DATE RECEIVED	GIFT DESCRIPTION	NOTE MAILED ✓
1.				
2.				
3.				
4.				
5.				
6.				
7.				
8.				
9.				
10.				
11.				
12.				

Baby Gifts

Flowers are arriving, the telephone is ringing and visitors are coming to see the new baby. This joyful chaos is full of mandatory daily tasks and treasured moments. Many moms and dads are exhausted, existing on adrenalin instead of sleep and fortified by the kindness of others. At the end of the day when the laundry is piling up and the baby may be sleeping, thank you notes are waiting. As a mother of two, it is my desire to make thank you notes easier for you to write, helping you to sincerely offer your heartfelt appreciation.

ETIQUETTE GUIDELINES FOR BABY GIFTS

1. Thank you notes should be written on informals or cards and signed with the mother's name, not the baby's name.
2. When good friends visit you in the hospital and bring you a gift, you do not have to write them a thank you note if you were able to thank them verbally in the hospital.

DATE

Dear Donna,

Thank you for the adorable yellow sleeper. It is so little and soft I know the baby will be very comfortable wearing it. I am looking forward to seeing you in the park, watching the children, and enjoying adult conversation. I appreciate your kindness, and you sharing this happy time with me.

Your friend,

Nancy

DATE

Dear Erica,

The colorful animal mobile was the perfect finishing touch for the baby's room. Rachel will love watching it move and listening to the music. As she gets older, it will keep her attention and ease her to sleep. Thank you for thinking of us with such a fun, decorative, and useful gift.

Fondly,

Nancy

DATE

Dear Aunt Lucy and Uncle Edward,

Thank you for the beautiful monogrammed silver cup. Baby Jason will enjoy the cup as he grows up and treasure it his entire life. You were so thoughtful to give him a gift that will become a family heirloom. Please come by and see him—he is growing like a weed! At his three month checkup he weighed 23 pounds.

We appreciate your thoughtful gift and are looking forward to Jason getting to know his great-aunt and uncle.

Love,

Nancy

DATE

Dear Margie,

The blue and white hat is darling. When we go to the park, Matthew will be warm and fashionable! I also appreciate your pediatrician recommendation and encouraging words. Thank you for the cute hat and sharing this happy time with me. I hope to see you soon.

Fondly,

Nancy

DATE

Dear Abby,

The blue and yellow baby blanket is beautiful. Thank you for such a pretty and practical gift. I will keep it handy on the rocking chair, so I can easily cover Julia while she naps. You were so thoughtful to tell me about the discount baby store. We plan to stock up on diapers and purchase a changing table.

I am looking forward to being a parent and sharing many more happy times with you.

Fondly,

Nancy

DATE

Dear Kathy,

Thank you for the beautiful baby book and traveling all the way from Boston to attend my baby shower. Since Mrs. Riley's fifth grade class, we have been best friends. We told each other our secrets, you helped me through math, and we cheered for each other to reach our goals. I hope my daughter, Allison, will be as fortunate as I have been, and have a friend like you.

I love the pastel colors and sweet ribbons on the baby book. We will treasure it always, filling it with happy memories. It was great to see you, and I will call you soon to hear more about Boston.

Love,

Nancy

DATE

Dear Aunt Rose,

Thank you for the delicious cookies and beautiful silver comb and brush set. The comb and brush set will look great on top of the baby's dresser. I am looking forward to dressing her up, and with your thoughtful gift I can comb her hair for a finished well-groomed look. I appreciate your thoughtful gifts and encouraging words. We are looking forward to being parents and sharing our joy with you and the rest of the family.

Love,

Nancy

DATE

Dear Aunt Celia and Uncle William,

Thank you for the beautiful Peter Rabbit dinner set. It is so cute and cheerful I am looking forward to using it as soon as Justin can hold a fork! He is sleeping longer at night so we are catching up on our sleep. Soon we would love to bring him by for a visit so he can get to know his aunt and uncle.

Again, thank you for your kindness and for sharing this happy time with us.

Love,

Nancy

DATE

Dear Robin,

Thank you for the silver picture frame. It is beautiful and perfect for my favorite picture of Bobby holding the baby in the rocking chair. I am looking forward to seeing you at Thanksgiving and introducing you to your new little cousin, Sarah. You were so thoughtful to think of us and send such a lovely gift.

Love,

Nancy

DATE

Dear Janice,

Thank you for the Disney storybook. It is beautiful. Virginia is a good baby, growing bigger every day and starting to smile. I know both of us will enjoy the bright colors and detailed illustrations when we read it together. I appreciate your kindness and sharing this happy time with us.

Love,

Nancy

DATE

Dear Aunt Mary,

Thank you for the jogging stroller. I love the idea of a chance to exercise while the baby is getting some fresh air. It is so sturdy we can go to the park with it or down the street. When the weather is warmer, Suzanne and I will be the first ones to enjoy the spring. We will use your generous gift for many years and think of you. I appreciate your kindness, and we are looking forward to sharing many more happy times together.

Love,

Nancy

DATE

Dear Mrs. Clayton,

Thank you for the adorable stuffed bear. The teddy bear is so soft and has such a sweet face, Brandon will love playing with him. We are lucky to have a great neighbor like you. Since we have moved next door, you have enriched our lives with kindness, cookies, and gardening tips. I hope you will enjoy watching Brandon grow up, and we will see you soon.

Fondly,

Nancy

DATE

Dear Mr. and Mrs. Simon,

Thank you for the savings bond for Martin. Your thoughtful gift will be used for Martin's college education. We love being parents, watching him grow and learn a little every day. He has an easygoing temperament and we hope he will be sleeping through the night very soon.

   We appreciate your thoughtful gift and look forward to seeing you soon.

Fondly,

Nancy

DATE

Dear Jean,

Thank you so much for the beautiful dress for Katheryn. I love the pink and yellow flower design, it is just perfect for a little girl. She will wear it for Thanksgiving next month, and I am sure she will be the belle of the ball!

We are looking forward to seeing you soon. I hope you and your family are doing well and will enjoy the holiday season.

Fondly,

Nancy

DATE

Dear Lindsey and Andrew,

Thank you for the darling outfit for Mason. He will look very handsome in the blue and white play clothes. The little ducks on the shirt are cute, and the blue matches his eyes. I cannot wait until he wears it to the park. He will be the best dressed baby there! I appreciate your kindness in celebrating the birth of our child.

Fondly,

Nancy

ORGANIZATION, ORGANIZATION, ORGANIZATION

	FROM	DATE RECEIVED	GIFT DESCRIPTION	NOTE MAILED ✓
1.				
2.				
3.				
4.				
5.				
6.				
7.				
8.				
9.				
10.				
11.				
12.				

$\mathcal{O}$RGANIZATION,
ORGANIZATION, ORGANIZATION

	FROM	DATE RECEIVED	GIFT DESCRIPTION	NOTE MAILED ✓
1.				
2.				
3.				
4.				
5.				
6.				
7.				
8.				
9.				
10.				
11.				
12.				

$\mathcal{O}$RGANIZATION,
ORGANIZATION, ORGANIZATION

	FROM	DATE RECEIVED	GIFT DESCRIPTION	NOTE MAILED ✓
1.				
2.				
3.				
4.				
5.				
6.				
7.				
8.				
9.				
10.				
11.				
12.				

Hospitality

How was your weekend?

When the answer was not what we hoped it would be, and we couldn't wait to leave, and we were relieved to be at home doing the wash, it is fair to say your weekend was not the best.

Jane, her husband, and two-year-old daughter Carolyn went to visit friends in Jacksonville for the weekend. Their friends were one hour late picking them up at the airport, and greeted them with hugs and a temperature update on their child's flu symptoms.

The adults did play golf and go out for dinner. Jane was amazed how well she played golf considering her back was totally out after sleeping on the foldout couch, and the small hyperactive dog had bitten her on the hand. On the drive back to the airport on Sunday, Carolyn vomited in the back seat, all over herself, her car seat, and her dad's carry-on luggage. They were able to return to Atlanta before the diarrhea and fever started.

The weekend could have been worse, so think of something positive to say and send a nice note to your host and hostess for their hospitality.

*E*TIQUETTE GUIDELINES FOR HOSPITALITY

HOSPITALITY IS AN ACT OF UNSELFISH KINDNESS. SOME-
ONE IS TAKING THE TIME TO TAKE CARE OF YOU. IF IT
ISN'T YOUR MOTHER, WRITE A NOTE.

1. Follow the general guidelines for writing thank you notes for gifts.
2. A note is required when you are spending one night or longer in someone's home (except for family or close friends) or when you are the
   guest of honor.
3. Every hostess or host enjoys receiving a thank you note expressing
   your sincere appreciation for his/her effort, kindness, and attention
   to detail.
4. Always describe the good time you had and the kindness you received.
5. When the hostess or host receives a gift, they should send a thank you
   note, especially when the gift arrives by mail or UPS.

DATE

Dear Mike and Patti,

We enjoyed staying with you in the Hamptons. From morning until night you entertained us, while at the same time making us feel right at home. We loved that little Italian restaurant where the bread was so good we had to reorder it twice!

Thank you for going out of your way to make our visit fun and relaxing. We enjoyed being with you and vacationing together. Enjoy the rest of the summer, and we will talk with you soon.

Love,

The Rutledge Family

DATE

Dear Alan and Diane,

Thank you for your kind hospitality last
weekend. Our trips to Pittsburgh are so busy
that it was a comfort to know your home
was waiting for us at the end of the day.

It was thoughtful of you to make sure we
started the day with a good breakfast. Your
pancakes with warm maple syrup were a
special treat. We appreciate all you did for us.
You really made your weekend houseguests
feel at home.

Love,

*The Wilson
Family*

DATE

Dear Aunt Lois,

The engagement luncheon was lovely. The Swiss Hotel provided a beautiful setting and the menu was delicious. I especially enjoyed the salmon salad, and as you know, pecan pie is my favorite.

You were so thoughtful to get together my friends and family to share this happy occasion. Everyone had a great time. Thank you for the luncheon in my honor and the happy memories all of us can share.

Love,

Gabrielle

DATE

Dear Lauri,

Thank you for dinner at the Bistro. Your choice of restaurants was great. The swordfish you suggested was seasoned and grilled just the way I like it. I am so glad we shared the chocolate dessert or I would have had to run an extra two miles!

Hearing about your ski vacation and travel tips made me want to plan a trip. The next time I go out west, I am going to call your travel agent for the best information.

Again, thank you for a most enjoyable dinner.

Best regards,

Betsy

DATE

Dear Mr. and Mrs. Johnson,

Thank you for the homemade coffee cake and for making us feel welcome in our new neighborhood. You were so kind to think of us. We had the coffee cake for breakfast this morning and enjoyed every delicious bite. We are looking forward to seeing you at the neighborhood 4th of July picnic and getting to know our other neighbors. Having thoughtful neighbors like you has made the transition to our new home easier and a pleasant experience.

Again, thank you for thinking of us.

Best regards,

The Butler Family

DATE

Dear Sally and Paul,

Thank you for bringing us dinner. The roast chicken, salad, mashed potatoes, carrots, and apple pie were a feast. We have been so busy with the new baby that we have not made it to the grocery store lately. Your thoughtful dinner was delicious and gave us the nutritional energy necessary to make it through a couple of days with our newborn and his three-year-old sister.

We are all doing well, just a little tired. Kevin and I appreciate your kindness and look forward to seeing you again soon.

Love,

Annie

DATE

Dear David and Debbie,

The two of you must be exhausted after last weekend. Every dinner, luncheon, and party was delicious and fun. I know you must be very proud of Josh. He did an excellent job reading from the Torah and greeting all the guests. You entertained us graciously, and we enjoyed being with you, your family, and your friends.

Thank you for the many details you thought of to make our weekend in Pittsburgh more convenient, comfortable, and a very good time. We loved seeing you and being part of Josh's Bar Mitzvah weekend.

Love,

The Goodman Family

DATE

Dear Harriet and Bruce,

After last weekend, I hope you were able to take a few days off work. The non-stop parties were great. We enjoyed everything from the Beef Wellington with champagne to the barbecue and beer! Jenny was a gracious and beautiful bride. Your new son-in-law, Jackson, seems like a mature young man who will bring pride to the family.

Thank you for making us feel welcomed and showing us a good time. We enjoyed being a part of your wedding celebration, and hope to see you very soon.

Love,

Olivia

DATE

Dear Anita,

The flowers arrived this morning and are beautiful. The multi-colored tulips mixed with sunflowers are dramatic, announcing the arrival of spring. I am placing them in the foyer where they will welcome all the dinner party guests. Keith and I are sorry you cannot join us tonight to celebrate Jennifer and Kevin's engagement. We will miss your interesting conversation and family insights.

Thank you for thinking of us, and we look forward to seeing you soon.

Love,

Barri

DATE

Dear Carolyn,

Thank you for including me last Saturday night and introducing me to all your friends. When you are new in town it can be hard to meet people in a casual and friendly atmosphere. Your St. Patrick's Day party was fun. I learned three new Irish songs and developed an interest in Notre Dame football!

I appreciate your generous spirit and friendship.

All the Best,

Margo

DATE

Dear Mary Beth and Eli,

We had a wonderful time with you last Thursday. The delicious dinner at Chez Maison and Broadway-style musical at the Fox Theatre were a real treat. Cathy Rigby's performance in Peter Pan was amazing. It was fun to be "taken away" by an entertaining show. You are gracious hosts, and we thank you for showing us Atlanta. Rick and I hope you will visit us in Chicago very soon.

Sincerely,

DATE

Dear Margaret and Brent,

What a weekend! We had a great time at your Hilton Head beach condominium. The ocean provided a playground for the children. Patti rested in the sun while she watched them from the beach. As you suggested, I played golf at Sea Pines and had a productive lunch with Ed Jenkins.

Thank you for the use of your beach home. We had a wonderful time.

All the Best,

Robert

DATE

Dear Rebecca,

Thank you for the beautiful box of Godiva chocolates. The package was so pretty, I hated to open it, but I could not resist the temptation. Every bite was delicious. The chocolate covered caramels and nuts were the perfect mid-day treat or after-dinner dessert.

I appreciate your thoughtful, generous, and loving spirit.

Love,

Aunt Georgia

DATE

Dear Carol,

Thank you for the amazing meal at your home last Saturday. The southern style barbecue was a sight to behold and a pleasure to eat. The large white tents protected us from the sun and provided a very comfortable place to enjoy the barbecue, corn, squash casserole, yeast rolls, and peach cobbler.

We had a great time listening to the music, seeing old friends, and meeting new ones. Travis and I appreciate your kind hospitality.

All the Best,

Grace

DATE

Dear Ashley,

Thank you for getting my mail and watering the plants. Knowing you were taking care of the house while I was out of town helped me relax so I could enjoy my vacation. Having a nice neighbor like you is one reason I like living in our community.

I appreciate your kindness. If I can ever return the favor, please let me know.

All the Best,

Charlotte

ORGANIZATION, ORGANIZATION, ORGANIZATION

	TO	DATES OF VISIT	FOR	NOTE MAILED ✓
1.				
2.				
3.				
4.				
5.				
6.				
7.				
8.				
9.				
10.				
11.				
12.				

ORGANIZATION, ORGANIZATION, ORGANIZATION

	TO	DATES OF VISIT	FOR	NOTE MAILED ✓
1.				
2.				
3.				
4.				
5.				
6.				
7.				
8.				
9.				
10.				
11.				
12.				

ORGANIZATION, ORGANIZATION, ORGANIZATION

	TO	DATES OF VISIT	FOR	NOTE MAILED ✓
1.				
2.				
3.				
4.				
5.				
6.				
7.				
8.				
9.				
10.				
11.				
12.				

Sympathy Notes
and
Acknowledgments

M<small>R.</small> B<small>ONNER'S DEATH WAS A SHOCK,</small> and saddened
Rachel deeply. She wanted to comfort her friend, convey her
sympathy, and help the family during this difficult time.
Rachel regretted sending a drug store sympathy card, but she
was at a loss for words.

ℰTIQUETTE GUIDELINES FOR SYMPATHY

FROM THE HEART, ABOUT THE SOUL, SAYING YOU CARE.
SYMPATHY NOTES ARE DIFFICULT TO WRITE. HOWEVER, THEY
MUST BE WRITTEN. THE SORROW YOU FEEL AND THE SYMPATHY
YOU WANT TO CONVEY CAN BE EXPRESSED IN A NOTE. YOUR
WORDS OFFER COMFORT AND WILL BE APPRECIATED.

1. Send notes as soon as possible.

2. Even if you send flowers, attend the funeral, or make a contribution, a sympathy note should be sent. However, if you personally and thoroughly offer your sympathy at the funeral, a note is not required.

3. The length of the note may be brief—a few lines or longer, depending on the relationship.

4. State the sad news of recent loss with the appropriate relationship. For example: "I was so sorry to learn about the death of your mother."

5. It is fine to say how difficult it is to find the words to express your feelings.

6. If the relationship is personal, include a personal thought. For example, "Sam had a great sense of humor, and he always knew what to say to make me laugh."

7. If you are sincere, offer help. For example, "I will call you next week to see what night I may bring you dinner."

8. In closing the sympathy note, offer comfort. For example, "Please know we are thinking about you and that you have our deepest sympathies."

DATE

Dear Anna,

I was so sorry to hear about the death of your father. You have told me on several occasions how smart and kind he was.

I know you will miss him and that this is a difficult time for you. I only wish I had the words that could ease your pain. Your loss is great, leaving an empty place in your heart and in your life. I hope your memories will give you comfort. I will call next week to see what day I may drive your son's school car pool for you.

You have my deepest sympathies.

Thinking of you,

Katheryn

DATE

Dear Mrs. Spensor,

I was very sorry to hear about the death of your husband. I worked with him at Becan Enterprises for five years. Ed was so knowledgeable about the product line, and easy to talk to, and he often helped me with sales information. He was always kind and patient, and he treated everyone at the office with respect. We will miss Ed's business advice, kind words, and friendship.

I am saddened by your loss. Please know you have my deepest sympathy.

With sympathy,

*Elizabeth
Johnson*

DATE

Dear Roberta,

I was saddened to hear about the death of your mother. Having met her on a couple of occasions, I know what a creative and interesting person she was. I was fascinated by her stories of growing up in Ireland and coming over to this country when she was twelve. Your loss is great, and I wish I knew the words to ease your sorrow.

Next week, after a lot of your family leaves, I will call to see what would be a good night to bring you dinner. Please know I am thinking about you and that you have my deepest sympathies.

With sympathy,

Christine

DATE

Dear Mr. Arlington,

Mrs. Greer, our neighbor, told me about the death of your lovely wife. I spoke to Mrs. Arlington several times at neighborhood events. At the last 4th of July picnic, she gave me helpful advice about how to improve the quality of my rose bushes. I often admired her garden, and she was so kind to share her gardening tips with me.

I am very sorry for your loss. Please know you have my deepest sympathy.

With sympathy,

Martha Singleton

DATE

Dear Maryann,

I was very sorry to hear about the death of your sister, Doris. This is a great loss for you and your family, and I only wish I knew the words that would bring you comfort. I hope the recent trip to England you shared with Doris will give you happy memories during this difficult time.

I am thinking about you, and please know that you have my deepest sympathy.

With sympathy,

Victoria

DATE

Dear Grace,

Your thoughtful note gave me great comfort. You touched my heart with your kind words and concern. During this difficult time, it is helpful to know I am not alone because of caring friends like you.

Fondly,

Robert

DATE

Dear Peggy and Sam,

Thank you for the contribution to the American Heart Association. Your donation means a lot to me, just knowing the money will go toward heart research.

In a few weeks, I will return to bridge club, and it will be nice to be with you again. I appreciate your kindness during this difficult time.

Best regards,

Marion

DATE

Dear Jill and Peter,

Thank you for the contribution to the American Cancer Society. It was so kind of you to remember George. The four of us had great times together. George and I often laughed out loud when we remembered that crazy dinner we shared in St. Thomas. He always enjoyed being with you, and I know we will all miss him very much. Knowing I have friends like you comforts me during this sad time.

Love,

$\mathcal{O}$RGANIZATION,
ORGANIZATION, ORGANIZATION

	FROM	DATE RECEIVED	NOTE MAILED ✓
1.			
2.			
3.			
4.			
5.			
6.			
7.			
8.			
9.			
10.			
11.			
12.			

$\mathcal{O}$RGANIZATION,
ORGANIZATION, ORGANIZATION

	FROM	DATE RECEIVED	NOTE MAILED ✓
1.			
2.			
3.			
4.			
5.			
6.			
7.			
8.			
9.			
10.			
11.			
12.			

Gift Index